Original title:
Oaken Odes

Copyright © 2025 Creative Arts Management OÜ
All rights reserved.

Author: Levi Montgomery
ISBN HARDBACK: 978-1-80566-718-6
ISBN PAPERBACK: 978-1-80566-847-3

Illuminating the Silent Sanctuary

In a quiet glade where birds all squawk,
The squirrels debate, while rabbits mock.
Sunbeams dance through branches overhead,
Even the mushrooms are out of bed.

A deer in boots struts by with flair,
Singing to trees, without a care.
The shadows giggle, secrets they keep,
While the trees whisper lullabies for sleep.

Reverence for the Timeless Timber

A wooden chair grumbles, ready to creak,
Roasted marshmallows in a game of hide and seek.
The logs tell tales of the wild and free,
While owls roll their eyes at the noise of the bee.

Bark-covered sages nod in delight,
While pinecones argue about the best flight.
A tree stump chuckles, wide and round,
As roots form a dance on the soft, rich ground.

The Whisper of the Wildflower

Daisies gossip under violet skies,
While buttercups trade their fashion tips, so wise.
A bloom lifts its head, shouting, "Be bold!"
While dandelions plan a heist for that gold.

Petals prance in a playful breeze,
Tickling the noses of busy bees.
Colors collide as flowers unite,
In a sprightly chaos, oh, what a sight!

A Pilgrimage through Leafy Labyrinths

Through winding paths of green and brown,
Explorers wander, never a frown.
A hedgehog holds a map upside down,
While crickets play tunes that make them dance around.

Beneath the ferns, they stumble and trip,
A frog offers snacks from its savory lip.
As acorns chuckle at the playful plight,
The maze of trees seems to wink in delight.

When the Wind Visits the Boughs

When wind does tango with the leaves,
The trees all giggle, they jest and tease.
Branches sway as if they chase,
Each gust a prankster in this leafy space.

The squirrels watch with laughing eyes,
As acorns tumble from high to the skies.
Branches bow, a bending ballet,
While the breeze plays tag all through the day.

The Legacy of Once-Wise Beings

Old trees chuckle with stories profound,
Of wise woodland creatures who once were crowned.
Their laughter echoes through decades past,
Reminding us how fun tales can last.

The owls hoot in a feathery jest,
While the hedgehogs consider their very best.
"Let's dance," they shout in a humorous cheer,
As the forest joins in, full of good cheer.

In the Heart of the Foliage

Under green canopies where secrets reside,
The plants whisper jokes, they take it in stride.
"Why did the twig refuse to dance?"
"Because it was stumped, no chance for romance!"

Fungi join in, with giggles galore,
Sharing puns as they sprout from the floor.
Nature's snickers mingle with the breeze,
Creating a chorus of chuckles and tease.

Songs Beneath the Bark

Beneath rough bark, funny tales grow,
Of tree stump meetings, where laughter flows.
"Knock-knock," says one, "Who's there, you ask?"
"A chipmunk who sings, no need for a mask!"

The saplings sway to a whimsical beat,
As the tall ones chuckle, shaking their feet.
In this woodsy choir, laughter does bloom,
Turning the forest into a bright room.

Journeying Through Leafy Portals

In the woods where the leaves do giggle,
Squirrels dance and the branches wiggle.
A rabbit jokes about trees so spry,
While mushrooms laugh as the clouds float by.

A frog in a bow tie croaks a tune,
To a chipmunk strumming under the moon.
With acorns rolling like marbles in play,
Nature's jesters brighten the day.

A deer in a tutu prances around,
While wise old owls just hoot, "What a sound!"
With each step forward, hilarity grows,
As the forest wears ticklish leafy clothes.

So join in the fun, take a stroll or two,
Past portals of leaves, where laughter's the cue.
In this goofy grove, there's joy to find,
Nature's comedy is one of a kind!

The Poetry of Petals and Pine

In the garden where the daisies wink,
The pine trees dance, they really stink.
Petals fall like confetti bright,
Squirrels party on a spring night.

Bees are buzzing a tune so sly,
While flowers gossip and laugh nearby.
Chasing butterflies with silly grace,
It's a nature rave in this funny place.

Chronicles Held in Knotted Grain

Once a tree said 'I'll grow not tall,'
Knotted wood, he took a fall.
He told his tale of twisting fate,
But ended up close to the gate.

Rabbits laughed, 'It's all in the bark!'
They gathered 'round as it grew dark.
Woodpeckers tapped a beat so sweet,
While squirrels danced with their tiny feet.

The Stillness Beneath the Stars

Beneath the stars, the crickets play,
A midnight concert, hip-hip-hooray!
The moon rolls over in fits of glee,
While owls hoot and pretend to flee.

Fireflies sparkle, twinkling bright,
They flash like disco balls in the night.
But frogs croak loudly, stealing the show,
They're the real stars in this funny glow.

Glimmers Amongst the Musty Ferns

In the forest where the ferns all grow,
Glimmers of laughter, they steal the show.
Mice in waistcoats do the cha-cha,
While raccoons host a big fiesta.

Beneath the fronds, secrets are shared,
Tales of acorns and how they fared.
With giggles echoing through the trees,
Life is amusing with whispers and tease.

A Symphony of Sap and Stone

Beneath the branches, a squirrel dances,
Its acorn cap is the latest fashion.
The trees chuckle, their leaves a-flutter,
While bees do the cha-cha, oh what a stutter!

Frogs in tuxedos croak a sweet tune,
As fireflies measure the light of the moon.
Mushrooms applaud in their fungi attire,
This woodland shindig, what a wild fire!

Sap drips like honey from a twiggy friend,
Nature's DJ spins fables, never to end.
The rocks tap their toes, a jovial crowd,
With roots playing bass, it's all quite loud!

So take off your shoes, join the delight,
In this merry grove, we dance through the night.
Each laugh in the forest, a symphonic tease,
Where even the bark grins, swaying with ease.

Vestiges of the Woodland Spirit

In a glade where the shadows tease the trees,
A spirit hums softly, stirring the breeze.
Whispers of mischief, giggles of glee,
With twinkle-toed fairies who sip chamomile tea.

Branches bend low, wearing hats that are silly,
While mushrooms debate if they're more than just philly.
Raccoons play poker, taking all bets,
While owls judge the game with wise little threats.

Acorns roll by like marbles in play,
As shadows spin tales of the forest ballet.
The laughter of critters mixes with leaves,
Crafting a symphony where every heart believes.

So tread with a grin, on this whimsical ground,
For vestiges linger, where laughter is found.
The spirit plays tricks, with a wink and a nudge,
In this leafy domain, there's never a grudge.

Pulse of the Ancient Realm

Deep in the woods, where old shadows roam,
The ancient trees find a vibrant new home.
They gossip like grandmas, their roots intertwined,
With tales of the past that are ever unlined.

A woodpecker taps to a rhythmic delight,
As mossy old logs hold a jam session night.
The critters all gather, in clusters and clumps,
While hedgehogs roll in, bouncing like lumps!

Twisted vines sway, keeping time with the beat,
As chipmunks all hop, with quick little feet.
The pulse of this realm is a curious tune,
Even the moon chuckles, peeking out at noon.

So if you should wander where wildness thrives,
Join in the laughter, feel the spirit of lives.
The echoes of joy are a tree's fondest dream,
Where every heartbeat makes nature's grand scheme.

The Sentinel Stands Still

Amidst the green, a sentinel glares,
With bark like a shield, it's seen all the stares.
Squirrels dare tease, while woodpeckers knock,
But the tree stands firm, like a leafy fort clock.

A rabbit hops by, wearing socks on its ears,
And giggles arise, dissolving all fears.
"Why do we stand?" asks the young sapling near,
"Because stillness is fun!" says the elder, sincere.

The wind spins around, sharing secrets galore,
As the leaves start to giggle, and laugh even more.
Playful whispers flutter, from twig to tall root,
In this quiet brigade, no one's a brute.

So stop for a moment, just look and enjoy,
The antics of nature, a joyful ploy.
The sentinel grins, with wisdom and cheer,
In the heart of the woods, all laughter is here.

Reflection in a Forest Mirror

In the woods, a twinkling brook,
Where squirrels flirt and creatures look.
The maple's shade, a grand display,
Says, "Don't just stand, come out and play!"

A mirror made of sun and trees,
Reflects a world that aims to tease.
The branches wave like jazz hands bold,
Swaying softly in the sunlit gold.

Whispers Among the Twisting Vines

Vines entwined like gossip queens,
Spreading tales of sweet routines.
"Did you see that owl's dance last night?"
"Oh please, she thinks she's quite the sight!"

They giggle low, a leafy laugh,
Sharing secrets on nature's path.
With every twist and playful turn,
The forest's jesters, we shall learn.

Shades of Verdant Serenity

In shades of green, the laughter spills,
Amid the ferns and gentle hills.
A frog in stripes declares his throne,
"Ribbit, ribbit, I'm not alone!"

The daisies nod, a witty crew,
In dappled light, they bicker too.
"Who tripped on me? That's quite uncouth!"
Said one, while grinning from her booth.

Echoes of the Woodland Whisper

In twilight's glow, the echoes play,
Chirping crickets join the fray.
"Hey ho, who's got the best tune?"
A woodpecker mocks, "I'm a boon!"

The whispers rise like bubbles pop,
Underneath the ever-crooked top.
Each creature claims their merry fame,
While nature giggles, sport in game.

Veins of the Timeless Earth

Roots dance beneath the ground,
Worms hold a funky sound.
Rocks play chess in silent nights,
While moles wear tiny crowns and tights.

A tree sneezes, drops some bark,
Squirrels laugh, it's quite a lark.
Old oaks gossip with much flair,
As pinecones fall like soft despair.

Gatherings in the Glimmering Shade

Underneath the leafy veil,
Beetles tell a funny tale.
Breezes swirl with a giggle,
As tree trunks start to wiggle.

Acorns roll like bowling balls,
While pine needles play in halls.
A rabbit joins with flair and wig,
With jokes that make the shadows jig.

Luminescence Amongst the Leaves

Fireflies dance like starlit sprites,
Making mischief in the nights.
Branches sway to a silly tune,
While owls hoot like a goofy loon.

Moonlight sparkles on a stream,
Reflections laugh, as dreams redeem.
The trees chuckle in delight,
As shadows prance and take flight.

The Guardian of Gathering Years

An ancient tree with a wise old grin,
Hides secrets and giggles deep within.
With every rustle, it shares a laugh,
Making squirrels snort through their half.

Branches wave like hands in cheer,
But watch out—there's a rogue deer!
It trips on roots with quite a flair,
Leaving echoes of laughter in the air.

The Fertile Soil's Secret

In gardens deep where veggies dwell,
The carrots plot and beans rebel.
Potatoes dream of being fries,
While radishes disguise their sighs.

The worms perform a wriggly dance,
While daylight stars in soil's expanse.
The lettuce giggles, green and vain,
As peas roll out their weather vane.

The cabbage sends its leafy spies,
To whisper secrets, oh so sly.
Tomatoes blush in red delight,
As beets declare, "We're outta sight!"

The soil's a stage, where growth is fun,
A comedy under the sun.
Each seedling tells a joke or two,
In this plot where laughter grew!

Nurtured by the Rooted Past

In humble beds where history sleeps,
The turnips hold their ancient heaps.
Old tales of roots with laughter ring,
As garlic sings of stinky bling.

The beets recall their colorful game,
While asparagaceae stake their claim.
Oregano chuckles in the breeze,
Sharing tales of wild, herb-y tease.

Potatoes dig for fame anew,
Claiming they once flew, not few.
Each sprout a jest of days gone by,
In this garden where giggles lie.

So listen close to leafy glee,
For every bloom holds history.
In roots we find our laughter's cast,
A quirky tale, long shall it last!

Triumph of the Life Force

A sprout takes arms to reach the sky,
While flowers bloom and butterflies fly.
The sun declares, "You shall not pout!"
As rain clouds gather, dance about.

The daisies cheer, in unison sway,
While dandelions shout, "Hooray!"
Their golden crowns, a sight to see,
As nature's jesters roam so free.

The life force laughs in every bud,
In muddy boots and garden crud.
Each petal holds a secret joke,
In every breeze, the gardens poke.

With roots that tickle underground,
And echoes of this joy abound.
Triumph sings through every leaf,
Nature's jest, beyond belief!

A Tapestry of Flickering Light

Underneath the moon's soft glow,
The critters dance, a lively show.
Fireflies twinkle in their attire,
As laughter sparks a wild choir.

The nightingale croons a playful tune,
While raccoons plot, beneath the moon.
A tapestry of bright delight,
In every shadow, giggles ignite.

The stars conspire with the trees,
As whispers drift upon the breeze.
Each branch a stage for prankster sprites,
A nocturnal fest of joyful sights.

So join the rhyme of night's embrace,
And let the mischief set the pace.
With flickering light and frolicking cheer,
A dance of nature, bright and clear!

Beneath the Timbered Sky

Under branches, squirrels play,
Chasing tales of yesterday.
Twigs gossip with the breeze,
Whispers of the laughing trees.

Acorns fall like tiny bombs,
With clever plots and grand charms.
Woodpeckers drum a silly beat,
While ants form parades on the street.

Sunbeams try to steal the show,
As shadows dance and crows say "hello!"
Nature's humor stitched in green,
A world where no one's ever mean.

Rustling Leaves of Wisdom

Leaves giggle in the autumn air,
Telling secrets without a care.
Branches shake with merry glee,
As nature serves a cup of tea.

Roots debate their lofty goals,
While nearby moss plays silly roles.
Fungi serve as comic relief,
Cracking jokes to hide their grief.

Windshowers laugh, tickling ends,
As nature sways and bends.
With every rustle, joy's unveiled,
A wise old oak just laughed and hailed.

Where the Rooted Dreams Dwell

In a world where dreams take flight,
Each green shoot a quirky sight.
Saplings giggle while they grow,
Sharing hopes of frosty snow.

Worms spin tales beneath the ground,
Of treasures hidden all around.
Beetles boast of their grand race,
While ladybugs share a warm embrace.

Dandelions blow jokes to the air,
Hoping they'll sprout everywhere.
Nestled roots with laughter swell,
In a kingdom where dreams dwell.

The Groves of Lost Memories

In groves where blossoms start to fade,
Old stories weave a girlish braid.
Echoing laughs of games well-played,
Fading softly as time invades.

Mossy seats from yesteryear,
Remembering laughter, joy, and cheer.
Each twig a witness, each leaf a friend,
Tales of mischief that never end.

Squirrels blush at their silly pranks,
As shadows dance in playful ranks.
Nostalgic winds sing sweet refrains,
In the woodlands where joy remains.

Chronicles of the Leafy Realm

In the realm where squirrels plot,
Acorns fall, and all is not.
A frog sings loud, a bird replies,
While ants march on, under the skies.

A tree stump holds a meeting grand,
With worms discussing weather planned.
The breeze whispers jokes, soft and sly,
As daisies laugh and daisies cry.

A snail with style, a shell of pride,
Slides past a hedgehog, too dignified.
They swap their tales of leafy dreams,
In a world that's bursting at the seams.

The sun rolls through, a golden egg,
While trees stretch out, their limbs like legs.
And here, amidst this playful spree,
Are laughter and joy, wild and free.

The Forest's Secret Lullaby

The nightingale sings a silly tune,
While fireflies dance beneath the moon.
A woodpecker laughs, peck-pecking away,
While bushes giggle at what they say.

A raccoon in masks steals a snack,
As rabbits hop with a daring quack.
The moonlight beams on this odd brigade,
Of critters who just can't be dismayed.

Mushrooms gather for a tea party fair,
Gossiping about who's got the best hair.
With each silly tale, their laughter grows,
In the woodland where the whimsy flows.

The crickets chirp a rhythm divine,
A lullaby brewed from sweet, wild thyme.
And if you listen, you'll surely find,
That laughter echoes through nature, unconfined.

A Canopy of Reflection

The leaves converse in chatter bright,
They gossip, giggle in morning light.
A squirrel acrobat flips with glee,
As sunbeams play tag on each leafy tree.

In the mirror lake, a frog strikes a pose,
While dragonflies twirl in sparkly clothes.
With each reflection, a chuckle is born,
As nature's jesters sing with the dawn.

A breeze dances through with a playful tease,
Tickling the ants on their busy knees.
The pine trees sway, with laughter they mix,
In a whirl of fun, they perform silly tricks.

And as day fades, stars come alive,
The forest giggles, the shadows thrive.
Under the night, in this leafy retreat,
Life's a comedic feat, oh so sweet.

Eclipsed by Shade and Sun

Under the sun's mischievous ray,
A bear tries yoga—what a display!
With a cat in a hat, they strike a pose,
The grass shakes its head, as laughter flows.

In the shade where shadows stretch and yawn,
A turtle complains: 'Where's my lawn?'
While butterflies plot their next big flight,
Pausing to chuckle at this silly sight.

A fox paints pictures with berries and leaves,
While a snickerling rabbit just barely believes.
As daisies dance, they spin around,
In the shade and sun, joy is found.

The forest buzzes with humor galore,
Where every tree is a comedian's core.
And here, with laughter shared in the wild,
Nature's comedy plays out, free and mild.

The Language of Bark and Branch

In the forest, trees do gossip,
Their whispers sound like silly flops.
They poke fun at the passing breeze,
While squirrels roll their eyes with ease.

A branch once told a joke so bad,
That even the leaves looked quite sad.
But the roots just chuckled underground,
Since they knew laughter knows no bound.

In the Stranglehold of Enchantment

A vine thought it could give a hug,
To an oak—what a silly bug!
The oak just shrugged, 'I'm far too stout,'
While the vine kept twisting around in doubt.

Mushrooms laughed as they sprouted near,
Saying, 'Look at that vine, full of cheer!'
'It hopes for a snuggle, but oaks are wise,
A growl from the bark is no sweet surprise!'

Shadows Dancing on Earth

Underneath the shadows, they sway,
A dance party for leaves, hooray!
With moonlight casting funny shapes,
The branches prance, the night escapes.

They twirl and spin, what a sight,
Saying, 'We'll dance until the light!'
But come the dawn, they sneeze and yawn,
'We'll nap on the grass, till the night is born.'

Balancing Between the Crown and the Root

There's a squirrel with a nut so grand,
Perched high in the crown, feeling quite spanned.
He wobbles and teeters, a sight to behold,
Laughing at ants, so brave and so bold.

The roots whisper, 'Stay grounded, dear friend,'
But he just chuckles, 'This fun won't end!'
With a flip and a flop, he drops his treasure,
And lands in a pile of leaf-wrapped pleasure.

The Ceremony of the Circling Seasons

Leaves gossip as they twist,
Acorns dance in autumn's mist.
Squirrels giggle, tales unfold,
Winter's blanket, cozy, bold.

Springtime flirts with fragrant blooms,
Bees wear tiny, buzzing costumes.
Summer laughs with sunlight's tease,
While crickets hum in evening's breeze.

Surrender to the Woodland Muse

The trees conspire with glee,
Whispering secrets to the bee.
Mushrooms wiggle, quite the sight,
As shadows play, they party all night.

A hedgehog dons a spiky crown,
As woodland creatures hop around.
The moonlight sparkles, jokes ignite,
In this forest, all feels right.

Under the Eye of the Moonlit Canopy

Beneath the beams of silver light,
Owl jokes with a mouse in flight.
Fireflies blink in playful raves,
While soft winds tease the forest waves.

Raccoons chatter, pots in hand,
Planning feasts across the land.
In shadows deep, a laughter flows,
The canopy, where humor grows.

The Sigh of the Sapling

A sapling dreams of skies so wide,
With every breeze, it sways with pride.
Giggles echo in its green embrace,
Longing for a squirrel's race.

Its roots tell tales of insects small,
Who tickle feet, they have a ball.
Reaching high, it waves to the sun,
In this wood, each day is fun.

Quietude in the Bark's Embrace

In the shade of leaves so wide,
Squirrels dance and run with pride.
A whisper speaks from knots and twigs,
While ants parade like bustling gigs.

A spider spins her web of dreams,
Conversations flow in funny themes.
The sun peeks through in golden glee,
As birds compose their symphony.

From Roots to the Stars

Roots dig deep in a comical way,
They gossip with worms through night and day.
Branches stretch like reach for fame,
While leaves tumble down, they have no shame.

The moonlight paints a quirky hue,
As critters giggle, the mischief crew.
They play chase with the twinkling skies,
In a game where no one is wise.

Adoration of the Aged

Bark that's rough tells tales of old,
Of squirrels bold and acorns gold.
With every ring, a secret spun,
Laughs and chuckles under the sun.

Mossy hats on ancient heads,
The trees sway gently, sharing threads.
They wink at passers with knowing bliss,
In nature's dance, they share a kiss.

Snippets of Nature's Serenade

Bees sing tunes as they buzz around,
Each flower's laugh is a joyful sound.
The wind tosses leaves in playful flight,
While frogs croak jokes all through the night.

Sunset giggles, painting the sky,
With colors bold, they shimmer and fly.
A dancing breeze whispers to the trees,
Of all their quirks that aim to please.

Whispers of Ancient Boughs

In the forest, trees do chat,
About squirrels and hats that sat,
One claimed to sprout a leafy crown,
While another just laughed and looked down.

Beneath the branches, shadows play,
Woodpeckers dance, then they sashay,
A acorn dropped on a raccoon's head,
And sent him scurrying, filled with dread.

The breeze carries tales of old,
Of branches swinging, bold and cold,
A cedar joked with a twisted pine,
"Your bark's so rough, it should sign a line!"

At dusk, the leaves like giggles sway,
As twilight turns the sky to gray,
The trees hold secrets, wild and free,
Of branches high and roots like glee.

A Symphony of Sequoias

In a grove where giants stand tall,
With each whisper, they seem to call,
A sprightly sapling joins the choir,
Singing loud about her desire.

"Hey there, ancient! What's your game?
A thousand rings, but all the same,
You grew so high, but what's the fuss?
Can you even hear the leaves discuss?"

A breeze collapsed with a tree-sized laugh,
As branches bent in a leafy gaffe,
The sequoias, bold with wisdom shared,
Exchanged their jokes, with laughter bared.

Underneath the starlit glow,
The forest floor began to flow,
With echoes of giggles, the fun amassed,
As the symphony played on, unsurpassed.

Echoes in the Canopy

In the treetops, where echoes dwell,
A parrot sings a jazzy spell,
"Hey squirrel, did you hear that pun?
You'd even laugh if you weren't on the run!"

Branches sway like dancers warm,
Each leaf swirls in a playful charm,
A chubby old owl blinked once, twice,
"Let's toast this nut, oh, wouldn't that be nice?"

The shadows play with ghosts of trees,
As whispers tickle the evening breeze,
"Who let the branches hang so low?
I tripped and fell; now I'm quite aglow!"

They chuckle about the way they bend,
How acorns tumble but never offend,
In this high realm of leafy jest,
The canopy laughs, a comical fest.

The Heartwood Chronicles

Gather 'round for a tale or two,
Of the heartwood's secrets, fresh and new,
A fig tree boasted, "I grow so sweet,"
While the oak just rolled its bark in defeat.

"Your fruit's nice, but wait till you hear,
The stories I've witnessed, year after year,
From drunken raccoons to sliding deer,
Heartwood's life, oh, let's all cheer!"

A whispering breeze made the leaves shake,
With laughter that caused a little quake,
"Your roots are old, and that's just fine,
But these shoelaces? Deer fashion divine!"

Every ring tells a story, it's true,
With chuckles shared by the aged crew,
From branches to bark, the wood hums sweet,
In the heartwood chronicles, where all compete.

The Veil of Moss and Magic

Under mossy hats, the critters play,
Spinning tales in a leafy ballet.
Gnomes sneak peeks with grins so wide,
While mushrooms giggle, sprouting with pride.

In storms they dance like it's their cheer,
As snails slide past, sipping on beer.
The fairies chuckle, with twinkling eyes,
While squirrels debate about pizza pies.

So let's join in this silly spree,
With enchanted glee, wild as can be.
A jig in the glen, come one, come all,
For who can resist a magical ball?

Resilience of the Timbered Giants

Tall trees boast with bark like armor,
Flexing muscles, growing ever warmer.
They laugh at storms with mighty roars,
While acorns drop like playful boars.

In the shade, a bird sings out loud,
Tickling twigs, making branches bow.
"Can you hear us?" the trees all chime,
"Life's too short; let's stop for a rhyme!"

With roots deep in crafty earth,
They hold secrets of laughter and mirth.
A dance with the wind, oh what a show,
As sunbeams cast shadows in an echoing glow.

Canopy Dreams

In the canopy, where dreams take flight,
Bouncing on branches, it feels just right.
Squirrels play tag with a feathery grace,
While owls keep watch with a wise, funny face.

Dappled sunlight creates a warm hue,
As creatures gather for a morning brew.
"Join us!" chants the vintage old cat,
"Let's spin some yarns and take a catnap!"

With whispers of breezes rustling the leaves,
Everyone giggles as mischief weaves.
A merry parade, sky-high with glee,
In the canopy, oh, how wild we can be!

The Language of the Leaves

Leaves gossip softly with every breeze,
Telling tall tales like old bumblebees.
"What's new?" asks the oak with a chuckle,
"Not much, just waiting for rain to trickle!"

Maples giggle, their blush never fades,
While willows weep in delightful parades.
"Let's start a song; we're sure to rock!"
The fruit trees hum, shaking their stock.

As shadows play tricks upon the ground,
Every swish of a branch is a giggling sound.
So lean in close, catch the leaf's little sigh,
For in leafy laughter, the worries all fly!

Secrets in the Shade

In the forest dark, a squirrel dances,
Hiding nuts while taking chances,
A cheeky grin, he winks to me,
Whispering tales of squirrel glee.

Under leaves where shadows play,
Rabbits plot a grand buffet,
Finger foods of clover green,
Guess their plans, it's quite the scene!

A wise old owl, perched on high,
Claims to know the reason why,
He hoots a pun with perfect style,
And leaves us laughing for a while.

So if you wander, take a glance,
At furry friends who love to dance,
For in this shade, so cool and light,
Laughter blooms, a pure delight.

Guardians of the Glade

In the glade, the toadstools stand,
Guarding secrets, oh so grand,
With mushroom hats, they hold a feast,
Inviting critters, every beast.

The hedgehogs gather, sharp and round,
With tiny glasses, they look profound,
Debating acorns like a show,
Who knew they'd be so in the know?

A deer prances, with style and flair,
Wearing flowers in her hair,
She strikes a pose, a fashion queen,
Next to her, a snail unseen.

So if you stroll through leafy lanes,
Join the dance of funny gains,
For in this glade of whimsy bright,
The guardians laugh from day to night.

When Branches Speak

When branches stretch and start to sway,
They whisper stories, come what may,
With rustling leaves, they share a jest,
Of woodland critters on a quest.

A quirky crow with glinting eye,
Tells of the day he learned to fly,
But misjudged a branch, oh what despair,
Fell in a puddle, flipping through air!

The willows giggle, swaying low,
With silly tales of seeds in tow,
They plot to root in neighbors' yards,
Turning gardens into bizarre cards.

So when you hear the branches chat,
Join in the fun; they're wise and fat,
In the symphony of leaves at play,
Laughing together both night and day.

Reverie of the Olden Wood

In the olden wood where dreams collide,
A fox discusses fashion with pride,
"Why wear the same bland coat all year?"
He questions styles without a fear.

The trees, they chuckle, old and wise,
"Have you heard of the raccoon's surprise?
He tried on hats from the human's trash,
And ended up making quite the splash!"

Beneath the branches, laughter roars,
As beetles argue about their chores,
Who has the strongest shell for battles,
Or who can best impersonate cattle.

So drift through stories, find your groove,
In the wood, where funny tales move,
For nature's laughter is wide and good,
In this reverie of the olden wood.

The Resilience of Rooted Souls

In the soil, they wiggle tight,
Dancing roots in morning light.
Worms play tag with giggles loud,
Trees stand tall, each feeling proud.

Squirrels boast of acorn finds,
While trees twist with playful minds.
Roots entangled, jokes afloat,
Who knew trees could sing and tote?

Whispers of the Ancient Grove

Leaves gossip in the gentle breeze,
Telling tales that make you sneeze.
Bark claims wisdom, yet goes blind,
Raccoons snicker, quite unkind.

The owls hoot with a knowing wink,
As chipmunks gather, munch and think.
In the shadows, shadows prance,
Branches sway, they join the dance.

The Heartbeat of Timber

Sap flows sweet in rhythmic beats,
Tree trunks sway with lively feats.
Beneath the knotted, gnarled skin,
Laughter echoes, hearts within.

Bugs brigade with tiny feet,
All join in for a wiggly treat.
Knots and kinks, each twist a grin,
Nature's joy, where life begins.

Beneath the Canopy's Embrace

Underneath the leafy quilt,
Squirrels draped in acorn guilt.
Fungi giggle, moss sways slow,
Shady friends in a leafy show.

When raindrops tickle, all take flight,
Dancing droplets, pure delight.
Roots rotund with tales to share,
Underneath, life's great affair.

The Soul of the Standing Behemoth

A tree in the park, so tall and wide,
Claims to be the king, with branches as pride.
Squirrels knock on its bark, a knock-knock sound,
They jest with each poke, old King Tree, so round.

With roots that trip joggers, a laugh in its bark,
It sways in the breeze, such a whimsical lark.
When autumn leaves tumble, they dance and they play,
The old giant chuckles, 'It's my party today!'

As bark beetles gossip, the whispers grow bold,
"Is that a crow's caw, or is it just old?"
The tree sways with laughter, it knows all the jest,
For nature's a stage, and it plays all the best.

So here's to the giant, who never seems shy,
With roots in the ground, and leaves to the sky.
A behemoth of joy, with a heart made of cheer,
Making shade for the picnics, year after year.

Journey through the Green Abyss

A walk through the woods, what a curious quest,
With branches that tickle and ferns, oh so dressed!
Each step is a giggle, a rustle, a cheer,
Nature's own playground, with nothing to fear.

The ground a soft carpet, in mossy green hue,
Where mushrooms do peek and say, "Please, have a view!"
Rabbits in top hats, dancing in style,
As birds chirp along, with a cheeky smile.

A stream filled with giggles, it bubbles with glee,
"Come play in my waters, be merry with me!"
Frogs wear their crowns, croaking witty tunes,
While turtles take selfies beneath sunny moons.

So let's wander freely in this green, jolly land,
Where every odd creature has something so grand.
The trees tell their stories, the flowers reply,
In the green, wacky world, randomness can fly.

Gazes Upon Gnarled Limbs

The old tree stands proud, with a twist and a bend,
Its gnarled limbs whisper tales that never seem to end.
Robins take turns to sit on its branches,
While woodpeckers giggle at silly tree prances.

As squirrels leap high, with acorn in tow,
They giggle and chatter, all ready to show.
"Look at my stash!" one proudly declares,
While the tree shakes its leaves, "Who needs all those wares?"

In winter, it shrugs off the snowflakes that cling,
"Is this fashion or folly?" it asks with a swing.
With humor so twisted, like its mighty form,
The old tree finds ways to keep spirits warm.

So here's to the limbs, both gnarled and aged,
With laughter and wisdom, so widely engaged.
For life's little follies are best when we share,
Under the shade of the tree, without a care!

Chronicles of the Evergreen Realm

In the realm of green, where the pines tickle skies,
Live creatures of whimsy, with bright, twinkling eyes.
The stories they tell, with a wink and a sway,
Are laced with mischief, come join in the play!

The owls wear their glasses, reading old lore,
While chipmunks hold court, sharing laughs at the core.
A pine cone parade, they march to and fro,
Claiming, "Here's the acorn! It's the star of the show!"

The sun rays burst forth, like confetti from dreams,
Bathing all creatures in glittery beams.
As laughter erupts, the trees join the jest,
In this evergreen kingdom, they're truly the best!

So raise up a toast in the woodland delight,
To tales of the forest that dance in the light.
For every green leaf sings songs fresh and bright,
In the chronicles woven by day and by night.

Verdant Testaments

In a forest where squirrels debate,
The oak trees chuckle, they think it's great.
With acorns falling like tiny bombs,
The laughter echoes through leafy psalms.

A raccoon in a hat plays the lute,
While singing to birds in sleek suits.
The foxes dance in a grand parade,
Complaining they're always the last to invade.

Dandelions bloom with pomp and flair,
As rabbits hop, without a care.
The whispers of leaves tell jokes unspoken,
Each giggle and grin, a friendship token.

In a circle of mushrooms, they host a play,
Where wildflowers act in a buoyant way.
The trees are the judges, with bark for the score,
And laughter erupts as they shout for more!

Guardians of the Ages

Beneath the boughs, the gnomes will fight,
For the best seat under the moonlight.
With comical hats and whispers sly,
They giggle at clouds that drift by.

A wise old owl, with glasses round,
Claims he's the smartest creature found.
But while he lectures on life and lore,
A squirrel snickers, and the branches roar.

The hedgehogs gather for tea by dusk,
Sipping from cups of the finest husk.
They tell wild tales of mischief done,
From chasing their tails to racing the sun.

In this woodland realm, the fun won't stop,
With trickster raccoons and a laughing crop.
Old trunks creak with each chuckle shared,
Proof that laughter thrives, for all who dared!

Resonance in the Hollow

In a hollow where shadows get bold,
The bunnies hop with stories retold.
Squeaky voices in joyful cheer,
As fireflies dance, drawing us near.

A family of crows holds a solemn event,
Debating what food makes the best dent.
But as they argue and flap overhead,
A pie in the sky leaves them all misled.

The turtles stroll, beneath big shade,
Sharing skin secrets they've often made.
With jokes about speed, they'll never lose,
They laugh at the thought of their slow-moving shoes.

In the quiet grove, the humor swells,
Where fables reside and laughter dwells.
Those roots deep in friendship, they twist and turn,
In nature's own laughter, we all can learn!

Echoes of the Long-Lived Trees

The old oak tries to tell a tale,
But his voice cracks like the bark, oh so frail.
With tales of storms and whispers of wind,
Even the ants start to chuckle and grin.

The bees buzz by, with plans of a dance,
Enticing the flowers to join in their chance.
But petals fall down, like confetti so bright,
Alas, a bee's fumble steals the night.

A wise tortoise boasts about his age,
While the younger ones roll, losing their gauge.
His sage words can't mask the giggles they share,
As they see him slip on his own tiny heir.

Underneath the twilight so splendid and fine,
The laughter of creatures, a jubilant sign.
For in each tree's knot and each leafy spree,
The echoes of joy are forever set free!

Reveries of the Ancient Grove

Beneath the leaves, where squirrels play,
Old branches whisper, 'Come what may!'
A fox in socks trots with a grin,
While laughing logs let the gossip spin.

The acorns drop like tiny bombs,
Startling birds with stealthy qualms.
Mice in capes hold a grand debate,
About the best way to serve a plate.

A tree stump claims it once was tall,
Now it just watches the critters squall.
Bark-covered tales of endless dreams,
Echo in twilight, like playful beams.

So join the dance in nature's hall,
The ancient grove is for one and all.
With every giggle and cheeky jest,
The roots of fun take a grand quest.

The Dance of the Dogwood

Under a bough, the flowers sway,
Dogwoods shimmy in bright array.
Bees wear hats and twirl around,
While grasshoppers leap in leaps profound.

A ladybug takes the lead,
With tiny shoes, it's quite the speed!
Twigs play tunes on a breezy flute,
As stems and petals join the pursuit.

Squirrels hold paws for a jig,
While shadows dance, oh that's quite big!
The bark claps softly along the beat,
Inviting all to join the feat.

So let's not wait by the old oak tree,
Join the dance; you and me!
Laughter rings through the boughs so wide,
In this merry waltz, let's take pride.

In the Heart of the Old Grove

In deep green folds of foliage wide,
A hedgehog sings with wobbly pride.
Chirping crickets join the tune,
Beneath the watchful autumn moon.

A chipmunk bets on acorn rolls,
While owls chuckle, sharing polls.
Trees gossip low in the evening haze,
Sharing tales of their ancient days.

A porcupine with a tutu twirls,
Creating chaos as it whirls.
Mushrooms giggle, they've heard it all,
Sprouting joy for the nightly ball.

So if you wander in this grove,
You'll find the laughter that trees have stowed.
With every chuckle and silly sight,
Your heart will dance through the starry night.

Sagas of Timbered Time

The oak stood sturdy, old and wise,
With branches stretching to the skies.
It tells of knights who rode their steeds,
While squirrels plot on secret deeds.

In sunlight's glow, a raccoon pranks,
Dressing leaves with style and thanks.
And every blossom has a lore,
Of who danced where, forevermore.

A crow in shades of midnight black,
Watches for snacks, it's quite the act.
His cawing tales of days gone by,
As fluttering butterflies pass by.

So gather 'round the trunk so grand,
Hear stories spun like golden sand.
In timbered tales, you'll surely find,
Laughter echoing in the mind.

An Arbor's Gentle Lament

In the breeze, I stand so tall,
Yet squirrels think I'm their great hall.
They scamper up, and munch my leaves,
While I just sigh and shake my eaves.

A chipmunk tries to take a nap,
On branches bent, he makes a trap.
I creak and groan from all the weight,
He dreams of nuts, I contemplate.

My roots are big, my trunk is stout,
But still get teased, oh what a pout!
For every twig that breaks in jest,
I nod my leaves, "I love this jest!"

So here I stand, a jester grand,
With acorn caps, I make a band.
The forest laughs, I join the fun,
All in good cheer, our day is won.

Songs of the Swaying Branches

Branches dance in sunlight clear,
Swaying gently, oh so near.
The robins chirp a tune so bright,
While I just wiggle in delight.

But oh! A crow, with beak so keen,
Floats by me, looking like a queen.
She squawks a tune, it's off the beat,
Yet still I groove on nature's street.

A windstorm comes, I lose my cap,
Twisted leaves in a messy flap!
Yet in the chaos, I find my cheer,
As foxes dance, we shed a tear.

The symphony of bark and breeze,
Brings laughter, driftwood with such ease.
Together we twirl, root, leaf, and song,
In harmony, we all belong.

The Arboreal Muse

In quiet woods where shadows play,
I'm inspiration, come what may.
With every knot and every bend,
My tales of whimsy twist, extend.

The bees debate on honey size,
While I just roll my wooden eyes.
A rabbit hops with carrot dreams,
And pulls a prank, or so it seems.

The owl hoots jokes, the bark annoys,
As busy critters trip—oh joys!
Yet here I stand, with roots all tied,
A sage of laughter, none can hide.

So come, dear friends, and take a seat,
Around my trunk, let joy repeat.
For every bark that breaks the rules,
Is just a note in nature's schools.

Tales from the Hollowed Trunk

In my trunk, a story flows,
Whispers of laughter, where time goes.
Inside this hollow, secrets lie,
Of foxes chasing butterflies.

Every knot's a tale I spin,
Of chipmunks plotting, and then some sin.
They giggle softly, beneath the moon,
While I just laugh in nature's tune.

A woodpecker knocks, what a surprise!
"Who's home?" he shrieks, with wide-open eyes!
"Just me," I chuckle, "and tales to share,
Of forest mischief and friendly dare."

So gather 'round, lend me your ears,
For stories wrapped in bark and cheers.
In hollowed depths, I find my joy,
A wooden heart, still a playful boy.

Threads of Light through Canopy

Sunbeams play tag with a leaf,
Squirrels take bets on who's the chief.
Butterflies giggle in midair,
While branches gossip without a care.

Mushrooms wear hats, oh so grand,
Fungi parties, a jolly band.
The sun spills laughter, a golden brew,
Nature's jesters have a ball, it's true.

A tree falls asleep, snoozing loud,
Bark hides secrets, wrapped in a shroud.
Feathers and twigs play dress-up too,
In the shade, a mischief crew.

So laugh with the leaves in the light,
Join the woodland, take a flight.
In the canopy, every spirit sings,
As nature shares its raucous flings.

Beneath the Dance of the Dappled Light

A jolly breeze tickles the grass,
While shadows waltz as they pass.
Sun and shade engage in a chase,
I swear, that tree just made a face.

The bunnies plot to steal some snacks,
While chipmunks chart their secret tracks.
Dappled laughs echo through the glen,
We're all silly, again and again.

Frogs take the stage, singing out loud,
Critters join in, feeling quite proud.
A beetle spins, the star of the show,
With winking eyes, it steals the glow.

So dance beneath this leafy dome,
Where every creature feels at home.
With giggles and wiggles, oh what a sight,
Nature's theatre, pure delight!

The Treasures of Tabletop Terrain

On a picnic bench, ants hold court,
Debating the merits of a cake fort.
Crumbs are treasures, a grand delight,
As seagulls plot their daring flight.

A thimble holds water, a lake so grand,
And tiny stick boats, built by hand.
Ladybugs race on a twiggy track,
While snails discuss their slow come-back.

Leaves are pages in this little tome,
Tales of adventure in their leafy home.
A walnut shell serves as a swap,
For acorn caps that make you hop.

So sit and share, a feast divine,
Under the sun, with nature's wine.
In this tabletop world, fun does reign,
With merriment, we'll entertain!

Embraces of the Fabled Trees

Who knew trees could be such a hoot,
With bird banter, they start to shoot.
'Look at my bark!' shouts the tall oak,
While the willow whispers a light-hearted joke.

Elves tease pixies, a race of charm,
Twisting around with a flirty arm.
Saplings giggle at the old folks' tales,
As wind weaves laughter through their gales.

A squirrel declares, 'I've lost my nuts!'
The wise oak nods, 'Yeah, life's a glut.'
With every rustle, a jest emerges,
Nature plays on, while humor surges.

So hug a tree, feel its hearty jest,
Join this world; it's simply the best.
In laughter and roots, we find our glee,
With the fabled trees, there's always esprit!

Memento mori of the Woodlands

In the forest's embrace, a squirrel hops,
Chasing its tail, it circles and stops.
The trees all chuckle at such a delight,
While birds drop their acorns, aiming just right.

A pinecone once whispered, 'Live life with glee!'
A chipmunk replied, 'Well, certainly!'
The rabbits laughed hard, rolling in weeds.
They dance with the wind, planting silly seeds.

But shadows grow long, the sun starts to wink,
The owl hoots a warning, 'Time's ticking, think!'
A laugh and a gasp, for all must decay,
Even the tallest will crumble one day.

So enjoy all the laughs, and gather the cheer,
For years keep on rolling, this much is clear.
The woodlands are wise, with humor so grand,
Let's giggle together, hand in furry hand.

On the Edge of the Leafy Threshold

At dawn speaks the sapling, 'I won't bend, no way!'
A leaf rolls its eyes, 'Oh, please, you'll sway!'
The grass cuts a joke, it tickles the roots,
While insects debate their fashionable suits.

The sun filters through with a giggle and beam,
A butterfly whispers, 'Nature's a dream!'
But falling from branches, a fruit took a chance,
And the ground erupted in a tango dance!

A wise old oak sighed, 'Feathers, not stone!'
Yet acorns were busy, in laughter, they'd grown.
With a twist and a flip, they tickled the air,
As everyone joined in a leafy affair.

So step on the edge, give laughter a whirl,
Let the wind be your partner, and give it a twirl.
At the threshold of green, where joys intertwine,
You'll find that the forest is simply divine.

A Memory etched in Leaf and Wood

Once carved in a tree was a heart that grinned,
With initials so silly, it hardly could blend.
A raccoon walked by, gave a curious glance,
'Did those lovers just trip? How'd they end up in romance?'

The bark laughed so hard, it shivered awake,
Recounting the moments, the pranks, and the cake.
A frog jumped in rhythm, croaking out loud,
Echoing tales that would gather a crowd.

As seasons would change, so swayed the old bough,
With memories sewn like fine stitching, it vowed.
Yet when winter arrived, and the lovers turned cold,
The heart swayed and crinkled with stories retold.

So next time you glance at a tree standing tall,
Remember the laughter, remember it all.
For life finds a way, in each leaf and each ring,
Etching memories sweet, like a joyful spring.

The Breath of the Bough

The branches above whisper secrets with glee,
They tickle the clouds, where no one can see.
A playful gust giggles, 'Catch me if you dare!'
While leaves drop like confetti, swirling through air.

The trunks chat of gossip, their bark rough and wise,
'Did you hear about the squirrel that thought it could fly?
A beetle shimmies, 'I danced on that bluff,'
But a twig gave a nod, 'Now that's just too tough!'

With each gentle bend, the boughs start to sway,
Declaring, 'Oh tree, it's a fun-filled play!'
The sun sets with laughter, its rays full of cheer,
While whispers of autumn float close, then disappear.

So join in the revels, take life as a jest,
Each breath of the bough tells us what we know best.
For humor's the heart of the green and the wood,
Embracing the joy, as only trees could.

The Grace of Gnarled Limbs

In the woods where branches twist,
A tree tried ballet, couldn't resist.
It stumbled and fell, with leaves all askew,
Now it waltzes with squirrels, and they giggle too.

With roots a bit tangled, the trunk full of knots,
It dreams of a life where it's not just in pots.
When winds come to dance, what a sight it must be,
A jolly old tree hosting a tea party spree.

The branches they wave, like arms in the air,
They tickle the clouds; do they really care?
They say that the birds hold a nightly embrace,
How funny they look with feathers and grace!

So next time you wander, just take a quick glance,
At trees doing tango, you might join their dance.
For nature is silly, it's vibrant and keen,
In the realm of gnarled limbs, joy's the routine.

In the Shadow of Giants

Underneath the tallest trees,
A chipmunk tries to tickle the breeze.
He leaps and he hops, full of bravado,
Saying, 'I'm the king! Just ask my shadow!'

The bark is so thick, it's quite absurd,
The trees gossip low, but they say every word.
'What's that little fella doing down there?'
A squirrel replies, 'Oh, just showing off flair!'

With acorns as jewels and leaves made of gold,
They crown tiny creatures, or so I'm told.
In the shade where the sunlight meets giggles and fun,
The giants stand tall, yet they never outrun.

So here's to the laughter, the humor so grand,
In the shadow of giants, life is well-planned.
Chasing down dreams like a butterfly's flight,
In a kingdom of gaffes, everything feels right.

Whispers of the Woodland Spirits

Deep in the forest, where the shadows creep,
The spirits of woodlands begin their heap.
With laughter like echoes and giggles galore,
They play hide and seek, behind branches and more.

A raccoon in a mask steals acorns with glee,
While a fox tells a tale of a flying bee.
The trees lean in close to hear all the hype,
As the stories grow wild, like an old campfire type.

They sing about mornings and that giant old snail,
Who once tried to race, but just left a trail.
With twinkles and winks, they hop on their way,
Causing mischief and cheer at the end of the day!

So wander on softly, and listen with care,
For whispers of spirits are floating in air.
With a heart full of laughter, let your spirit roam,
In the woodland's embrace, you'll always feel home.

Legacy of the Leafy Realm

In the leafy realm of folly and fun,
A family of hedgehogs is on the run.
Rolling and tumbling, they race through the grass,
They swear they're Olympic; but oh, what a pass!

With thorns for their armor, they laugh and cheer,
Each bump on the head reveals a new fear.
The trees crack a smile, their branches all sway,
As they drum up a tune for the hedgies at play.

In a leaf-covered castle, a badger presides,
With crowns made of daisies, his humor abides.
He jests that his rule is a tad bit askew,
When his subjects insist they're the ones who grew!

So cherish the laughter that echoes and streams,
In the legacy leafy, where mischief redeems.
For every small creature, so funny and bright,
In the realm of the leaves, they'll dance till the night!

www.ingramcontent.com/pod-product-compliance
Lightning Source LLC
Chambersburg PA
CBHW051638160426
43209CB00004B/707